Amish
Proverbs

Amish Proverbs

Words of Wisdom
from the Simple Life

EXPANDED EDITION

Suzanne Woods Fisher

Revell

a division of Baker Publishing Group
Grand Rapids, Michigan

© 2012 by Suzanne Woods Fisher

Published by Revell
a division of Baker Publishing Group
P.O. Box 6287, Grand Rapids, MI 49516-6287
www.revellbooks.com

Portions previously published 2010 as a gift book by Revell

Printed in the United States of America

Library of Congress Cataloging-in-Publication Data
Fisher, Suzanne Woods.
    Amish proverbs : words of wisdom from the simple life / Suzanne Woods
Fisher.
        pages cm
    Includes bibliographical references.
    ISBN 978-0-8007-2096-4 (pbk.)
    1. Conduct of life. 2. Amish—Conduct of life. 3. Aphorisms and apothegms.
I. Title.
    BJ1589.F57 2012
    289.7′3—dc23   2012022067

To protect the privacy of those who have shared their stories with the author, some names and details have been changed.

The internet addresses, email addresses, and phone numbers in this book are accurate at the time of publication. They are provided as a resource. Baker Publishing Group does not endorse them or vouch for their content or permanence.

12   13   14   15   16   17   18   7   6   5   4   3   2   1

In keeping with biblical principles of creation stewardship, Baker Publish-ing Group advocates the responsible use of our natural resources. As a member of the Green Press Initia-tive, our company uses recycled paper when possible. The text paper of this book is composed in part of post-consumer waste.

To my mother, Barbara Benedict Woods,
who raised her children
on Pennsylvania Dutch sayings.
This one is her favorite:

"Every mother crow thinks her own little crow is the blackest."

Contents

Acknowledgments

These collections are drawn, with permission, from a variety of sources: *The Sugarcreek Budget*, *Proverbs of the Pennsylvania Germans* by Dr. Edwin Miller Fogel, the *Pennsylvania German Dictionary* by C. Richard Beam, and the sayings and adages I grew up hearing from my grandfather's Old Order German Baptist Brethren family.

My grandfather—we called him Deardad—was famous for pointing out to me with a frown that "young folks should use their ears and not their mouths."

Another saying I grew up hearing was, "Choose your love and love your choice." That one belongs to my mother.

Introduction

The Amish in Their Own Words

Most every culture has proverbs that are unique to it. Whether called maxims, bromides, truisms, idioms, expressions, sayings, or just an old saw, proverbs are small, concentrated packages that let us peek into the window of a people's values and beliefs. They give us insight into a culture, its faith, folklore, history, language, mentality, psychology, worldview, and values. These pithy sayings are not meant to be universal truths. They contain general observations and experiences of humankind, including life's multifaceted contradictions.

"Proverbs," radio Bible teacher J. Vernon McGee once said, "are short sentences drawn from long experience."[1]

The ancient Eastern world—Egypt, Greece, China, and India—is thought to be the home of proverbs, dating back to collections from as early as 2500 BC. King Solomon, who reigned in the tenth century BC, gathered many of them from other sources as well as edited and authored others. Over five hundred were compiled into the book of Proverbs in the Bible. Proverbs were used in monasteries to teach novices Latin. Often colorfully phrased, at times even musical in pronunciation, proverbs served as teaching tools for illiterate populations that relied on oral tradition.

Interestingly, the proverbs have played a surprisingly prominent role in the speech of the Pennsylvania Germans, which includes—though isn't limited to—the Amish. "It is natural that the Pennsylvania Germans should use the proverb extensively," writes Dr. Edwin Miller Fogel in his book *Proverbs of the Pennsylvania Germans*, "because of the fondness of the Germanic peoples for this form of expression. The proverbs are the very bone and sinew of the dialect."[2]

"The ones that are common in the community are most likely in the oral tradition," says Dr. Donald B. Kraybill, senior fellow at the Young Center for Anabaptist and Pietist Studies at Elizabethtown College, Pennsylvania. "Not particularly Amish, but part of the broader rural tradition of the area."[3]

The Pennsylvania Deitsch dialect (which is called "Penn Dutch," though it has no relationship to Holland) originated in the Palatinate area of Germany over four hundred years ago and was brought to Pennsylvania in the 1700s with a wave of immigrants: Lutherans, Mennonites, Moravians, Amish, German Brethren, and German Reformed. Penn Dutch was, and is, an oral language; even today, people from different states can understand one another since the language has remained close to its origins.

"Most of what they [German immigrants] knew, they brought here from the Old World," explains C. Richard Beam, retired full professor of German at Millersville University. "The proverbs were an integral part of Pennsylvania German culture. The further back you go, the richer the language."

The cleverness of a proverb, though, can be lost in translation. Here's an example: *Wer gut Fuddert, daer gut Buddert.* "Good feed, much butter." Here's one that comes through a little smoother: *Bariye macht Sarige.* "Borrowing makes sorrowing."

Beam worries that the language has been watered down and diluted over this last century, as the external culture has crowded out its rich heritage. Raised in Pennsylvania, Beam says that all four of his grandparents spoke Deitsch as their first language. "We spent time with aunts and uncles and grandparents. That led to a richness of the culture, a preservation of the language. This was prior to radio and television." Beam is now 84 years old. "There's a saying I was raised with: 'Every time the sheep bleats, it loseth a mouthful.' That applies directly to the culture today." The dialect is losing words, he says. "Language doesn't stand still."

Today, only the Old Order Amish and the Old Order Mennonites have retained Deitsch as their first language. The Old Order Amish is a society that does not permit higher education. Theirs is a culture learned from the simplicity of their ancestors' lifestyles, and the Amish value this heritage. This simple lifestyle, passed virtually unchanged through the generations, provides an ideal base for the continual use of proverbs.

Within the last century, the use of proverbs in modern American society may have diminished, but not so for the Amish. In fact, the opposite is happening.

The Sugarcreek Budget is a weekly newspaper for the Amish-Mennonite community that began in 1890. Scribes from all over the world send in a weekly letter to the Ohio headquarters. At the end of most letters, a proverb is added, like a benediction. "The trend began about five to eight years ago," explains editor Fannie Erb-Miller. "We started to allow a saying on the end of a scribe's letter, and then it just caught on. Now, almost all of the letters have one. Early on, letters didn't include them. Mostly, they're sayings that pass from generation to generation. The proverbs are very relevant. They can speak to you. They can hit you."

The proverbs in this book, like all proverbs, come from many sources—most of them anonymous and all of them difficult to trace. It is not unusual to find the same proverb in many variants. The saying "Bend the tree while it is young; when it is old, it is too late" is a variation on the Bible's "Train up a child in the way he should go: and when he is old, he will not depart from it" (Prov. 22:6 KJV).

God plays a prominent role in Amish proverbs, as does nature: weather and seasons, agriculture and animals. In our modern world, the rural savvy may seem outdated. But look a little deeper. The proverbs are every bit as relevant in the year 2012 as they were in 1712: *Der alt Bull blarrt als noch* means "The old bull keeps on bellowing," or to give it a twenty-first-century twist, "The old scandal will not die down."

These sayings and proverbs, dear to the Amish, can help the English (non-Amish) better understand them. For example, here are two proverbs that reveal how the Amish value the virtue of patience: *"Only when a squirrel buries and forgets an acorn can a new oak tree come forth,"* and *"Adopt the pace of nature; her secret is patience."*

Proverbs are just as useful in our life today as they are to Old Order Amish families. They're just as relevant to us as they were to the Israelites in King Solomon's day. They help point us toward wisdom, toward good judgment, toward God's teachings. To please God, we must know what he values: What does he care about? What does he love? What does he hate? Proverbs teach us about God.

That is the ultimate goal of the proverb: to help others learn by experience and live wisely, pleasing to God. By perpetuating these same phrases, we constantly remind ourselves of their importance and their power to prevent us from forgetting the lessons they hold.

One thing is certain: there is no such thing as a simple proverb.

Time

---◼---

*Don't hurry, don't worry, do
your best, leave the rest!*

---◼---

Linda sat with her son in the emergency room of their local hospital, waiting to be seen by a doctor. Her son had twisted his ankle playing a game of basketball, and she worried he might have caused serious damage to it.

After ten minutes, her son grew fidgety and impatient. "This is going to take forever," he moaned.

Seated across from them was a young Amish couple. The wife had taken a spill and hurt her shoulder. They sat calmly, though Linda noticed the wife wince in pain whenever she shifted in her seat. Finally, the nurse came out and motioned to the Amish man.

He jumped up to help his wife rise to her feet. Linda heard him say to her, "Now, Katie, that wasn't too bad a wait. Only an hour."

After the Amish couple left the waiting room, Linda nudged her son with her elbow. "Do you see the difference? You expected to be seen immediately. They expected to wait."

To the Amish, waiting isn't a verb. It's an attitude. They wait for spring to plow and plant, for autumn to reap and harvest. They know that the seasons can't be rushed. They wait for the rain to come and nourish their crops. Much of their three-plus-hour church service is a time of silent waiting: they wait in expectation before God, rich with the promise of what is to come.

"Rest in the LORD, and wait patiently for Him" (Ps. 37:7 KJV) is a biblical principle the Amish take to heart. Waiting on the Lord is the same thing as trusting him. All that they have belongs to him, including the minutes and hours and days and years that make up their lives.

Time is just viewed differently for the Amish than for the English. It's not as important.

"In Indiana," says Dr. Joe Wittmer, raised in an Old Order Amish home, "the English move their clocks forward an hour in the spring and back an hour in the fall, but we never moved ours forward or back at any time. We went by 'sun' time and I don't remember being concerned about what time it was. Time was not important and we had only one clock in the house and it wasn't running most of the time. We based our time on 'sun up,' 'noon,' and 'dark' time."[1]

The Amish recognize patience as a key part of God's character. Conforming their will to God's will is what being Amish is all about. One way they try to conform is to purposefully slow down the tempo of life—an obvious example: they ride in a buggy pulled by a horse.

"We were never in a hurry," says Dr. Wittmer. "It's difficult to be in a hurry in a horse and buggy."

They have a deep connection to the rhythms of nature through their farm, even if it's just a few acres to grow their own fruits and vegetables. They eschew time thieves: television, radio, newspapers. It's as if they live their life with an unlimited amount of time, as if they have a toe in the door to eternity.

Common sayings promote patience as a virtue:

*It takes a century for God
to make a sturdy oak.*

———

Harvest comes not every day.

———

*A handful of patience is worth
more than a bushel of brains.*

———

You can't make cider without apples.

———

Don't count your eggs before they are laid.

19

What a contrast to the English perception of time: there's never enough of it! Time is viewed as an enemy or, at the least, as an irritating constraint. We try to beat the clock, and use technology or machinery to speed up tasks. In an ironic twist, time seems even more elusive despite more gadgetry that promises us more spare time.

The Amish can teach us to slow down. Time is not something to be mastered but a boundary to be respected. They remind us that Christians should look at life from a different perspective because we are part of a different kingdom—one that stretches into infinity.

"Run the race with eternity in view" and "What we do in this life echoes in eternity" are frequently quoted in sermons. And one thing the Amish know to be true: unlike humans, God is not in short supply of time. There is no limit to his days or his patience or his joy.

*Morning does not dawn with
the first bird's song.*

---

*If you keep waiting for the right time,
you may never begin.*

To stay youthful, stay useful.

You only live once, but if you
work it right, once is enough.

———■———

Many times we are climbing mountains
when we ought to be quietly resting.

———■———

Do more of less.

———■———

The years can fly past like a flock of birds.

———■———

One thing you can learn by watching
the clock is that it passes time
by keeping its hands busy.

———■———

21

We move forward, into the
future, one day at a time.

———◼———

Patience is a virtue that carries a lot of wait.

———◼———

In autumn sunshine,
prepare for winter's cold.

———◼———

A task takes as long as it takes.

———◼———

Regrets over yesterday and the
fear of tomorrow are twin thieves
that rob us of the moment.

———◼———

Enjoy today . . . it won't come back.

———◼———

You can't make good hay from poor grass.

———■———

*Live each short hour with God and the
long years will take care of themselves.*

———■———

To master this life, spend time with the Master.

———■———

*This would be a wonderful world if people
showed as much patience in all things
as they do in waiting for a fish to bite.*

———■———

*Today has one thing in which all of us
are equal: time. All of us drew the same
salary in seconds, minutes, and hours.*

———■———

23

*The person who kills time has
not learned the value of life.*

———————————

No time is lost waiting on God.

———————————

*There's only a heartbeat between
time and eternity.*

———————————

*Worry wastes today's time,
cluttering tomorrow's opportunities
with yesterday's troubles.*

———————————

*Beware of the barrenness
of a too-busy life!*

———————————

If you wish to be happy,
we'll tell you the way:
don't live tomorrow till you've lived today.

———■———

What we are when we are old is what
we learned when we were young.

———■———

The only preparation for tomorrow
is the right use of today.

———■———

Things that steal our time are
usually the easiest to do.

———■———

What a new year brings us depends a great
deal on what we bring to the new year.

———■———

25

One of these days is none of these days.

———■———

Memories are a keepsake no one can steal.

———■———

Hold tight to what is eternal and
loosely to what is temporal.

———■———

Cooks and bakers know the secret
to a good day is patience.

———■———

Don't worry what you could do if you lived
your life over; get busy with what's left.

———■———

Constant change is here to stay.

———■———

Life in the fast lane is normally a blur.

Money

Those who would have money are troubled about it, those who have none are troubled without it.

A few years ago, I called an Old Order Amish farm in Pennsylvania to make a reservation to stay for a trip I had planned. I left a message on an answering machine and received a return call just a few hours later from a woman named Viola Stoltzfus. Viola called from the phone shack down the lane from her farm. Every few minutes, her gentle voice—with just a trace of an accent—was drowned out by the clip-clop sounds of a horse and buggy passing by. After Viola wrote down the dates of my visit, I asked her how much money I should send to reserve the room.

"Well," she said, "we're too busy to make a breakfast for you. So, just send me a donation."

Nonplussed, I had absolutely no idea how much to send, so I wrote out a check for the amount I was spending at an airport hotel the night before. As I sealed that envelope to Viola and stuck a stamp on it, I couldn't remember ever feeling so good about writing someone a check. Why? Viola offered me two things that are in short supply in a secular world: She wasn't trying to unduly profit off of my visit but to receive a fair exchange for goods and services. And she trusted me to decide what that would be worth.

"As the work, so the pay," goes the saying.

It's not that the Amish aren't money savvy; they are. But their goal in life isn't to accumulate wealth. Money is a tool, not a goal. They want only to support their family in an environment that best reflects their values. They believe in ownership of land, hard work, frugality, honesty, and industry. But they strive to prevent affluent living, keeping up with the Joneses, and social status. In fact, they don't even value the indicators of success that we prize: income, education, luxuries, and symbols of prosperity. To the Amish way of thinking, *"If fools have much, they spend much."*

Many proverbs warn of the dangerous effects of affluence: corruption, laziness, friendlessness. Suspicion surrounds wealth. Many proverbs reflect this mistrust:

The rich are poor payers.

Where there's money, you'll find the devil.

———— ■ ————

A full purse never lacks friends.

Instead, the Amish give their highest respect to those who care well for their homes and families and community, those who raise their children so they will grow up wanting to become Amish, and those who help the next generation settle on farms. *"It is a wealthy person, indeed, who calculates riches not in gold but in friends."*

The Amish put the brakes on accumulation and all of the distractions and complications that come with it. There's a point where enough is enough, especially if it interferes with what is truly important to them: faith, family, community. That's where they draw the line.

Enough is enough is a rare concept for our modern world. A curious finding by a 2009 study shines a spotlight on one result of affluence: the higher the income, the less time a family spends together.[1] The decline in family time, the study found, coincided with a rise in Internet use and the popularity of social networks. The study found that, whether it's around the dinner table or just in front of the television, American families are spending less time together.

The Amish remind us that there is goodness and satisfaction in a simpler life.

Where is your line drawn? When is enough, enough?

What is not worth thanking for
is not worth having.

Soon got, soon spent.

Those who let God provide
will always be satisfied.

A person may hoard up money,
he may bury his talents,
but you cannot hoard up love.

Money talks, but it doesn't say
when it's coming back.

You get what you pay for.

---

*If you're careful with your pennies,
the dollars will take care of themselves.*

---

*He who has no money is poor; he who
has nothing but money is even poorer.*

The debt that is paid is best.

---

*You are only poor when you
want more than you have.*

Penny wise, pound foolish.

Where love is, there riches be,
keep us all from poverty.

———■———

Fortune knocks once,
but misfortune has more patience.

———■———

Thoughts are tax-free.

———■———

An industrious wife is the
best savings account.

———■———

Generosity leaves a much better
taste than stinginess.

———■———

*It's not what you make but what you
save that gets you out of debt.*

———————■———————

*That which controls your heart
controls your life.*

———————■———————

*It is worse to have an empty purpose
than it is to have an empty purse.*

———————■———————

*If you want to feel rich, just count the
blessings that money can't buy.*

———————■———————

*Statistics show that women spend
85% of the consumer dollar,
children 15%, and men the rest.*

———————■———————

Wisdom enables one to be thrifty
without being stingy, generous
without being wasteful.

———■———

Most folks tend to forget that
even a bargain costs money.

———■———

How we spend Christmas is of greater
significance than how much we spend for it.

———■———

Poverty and health are better
than sickness and wealth.

———■———

Money burns a hole in the pocket.

———■———

*Loving does not empty the heart,
nor giving empty the purse.*

---

*The boy who gave the loaves and
fishes didn't go hungry.*

---

*The values we leave our children
are more important than the
valuables we leave them.*

---

*Jesus wants to be Lord over our thoughts,
words, deeds . . . and wallets.*

---

*There are two kinds of leaders: those
who are interested in the flock, and
those who are interested in the fleece.*

---

*If money could buy happiness, people
would still wait till it went on sale.*

———■———

*The blacksmith's horses are
always shod the worst.*

———■———

*Every spiritual investment will
bear eternal interest.*

———■———

*It is better to be short on cash
than short on character.*

———■———

The devil dances in an empty pocket.

———■———

Money does not go as far as it used to,
but it's just as hard to get back.

———■———

Letting go of earthly possessions enables
us to take hold of heavenly treasures.

———■———

One man's money is as good as another's.

———✳———

A loaded wagon creaks,
an empty one rattles.

———✳———

To be poor is not disgraceful but unhandy.

Faith

A happy life and eternal salvation
is spoiling the devil's calculation.

ary Miller is a thin, attractive Amish woman of 46, a mother to eight children born within a span of eleven years. During the day, Mary wears a starched white organza prayer cap over her tightly pinned hair bun. In the night, she wears another covering. Why does she wear a head covering at night? "In case I wake up in the night and need to pray," Mary explains in a tone that suggests it should be quite obvious. "And with eight children, I do. Often."

Religion is 24/7 for the Amish. Everything they do, especially the manner in which they dress, is based upon their faith. Their simple clothing—a tradition of the Amish and the reason they are also called the Plain People—is a tangible reminder that they are a people set apart, belonging to the Lord. The *Kapp* or "head cap," worn by every woman and even by infants, might be the most symbolic garment of all. As girls become young teens, they start to wear the cap: black for Sunday dress and a white cap at home. After marriage a white cap is always worn. The style and size of caps can vary among church districts, but it is essentially the same cap as that worn by the Palatine women of the seventeenth and eighteenth centuries. Back in those days, the Amish were perceived as radicals.

To a modern world, the Amish still seem radical. Their deep commitment to faith is why they choose to live separate from the world. They believe the ways of the world oppose God. They eschew accumulating materialistic goods because it leads them to pride. Their Plain clothes serve to keep them separate from the world by creating a unifying identity. Their dependence on a caring community is intended to reflect the body of Christ. Their emphasis on humility reminds them that God alone is worthy of praise. Try to pay an Amish person a sincere compliment and you will most likely get a soft-spoken deflection in return: "Oh, I don't know about that."

The Amish take temptation to pride very seriously. "Because of our tendency toward pride," says David Miller, Mary's husband, "we need the cross, the Spirit, and the example of Christ." The Lord's Prayer holds great meaning to the Amish and in it Christ's petition: "Lead us not into temptation, but deliver us from evil."

The admonition of Proverbs 16:18, "Pride goes before destruction, a haughty spirit before a fall," is taken seriously by the Amish. Many proverbs warn of pride that leads to disaster:

"The crowing hen comes to no good end" is pretty clear.

"Nothing in front and nothing behind" means a person is proud and has nothing to be proud of.

David has made a lifelong practice of memorizing Scripture. He likens the Scriptures to "plumb bobs"—the weight that always holds a builder's plumb line straight and true. David seeks to measure his own thoughts, feelings, and behavior by God's Word—regardless of the circumstances. "Standing your ground is easier," he says, "when you are grounded in God's Word."

Most Amish believe the adage that "The cornerstone of faith is truth, not tolerance." They take Scripture literally and don't rationalize or justify behaviors that the Bible labels as sin. Evil is evil, and the source of evil is the devil, for whom they have a healthy respect. Traditional sayings make the devil sound active and nearly ever-present:

*Speak of the devil and you'll
hear the flop of his wings.*

---

*You need not call the devil,
he'll come without calling.*

And no one is immune to temptation: *"Even a saint is tempted by an open door."*

But the focus of the Amish life is not solely on avoiding temptation. It is on pleasing God, conforming to his will, living a faithful life, and hoping for an eternity in his presence. After all, to their way of thinking, "The best way to escape evil is to pursue good."

Bibles that are coming apart
usually belong to people who are not.

It may be difficult to wait on the Lord,
but it is worse to wish you had.

He who bows lowest in the presence of God
stands straightest in the presence of sin.

Faith is the bridge over which we can cross
all the unknown waters of tomorrow.

In creation, God spoke and it was so. He
used his finger to deal with the devil and
he made bare his mighty arm to save us.

---

*You can't stumble when you
are on your knees.*

———■———

*God speaks to those who
are quiet before him.*

———■———

*Faith in God is like a kite—
a contrary wind only raises it higher.*

———■———

*A heart at peace
gives life to the body.*

———■———

*When fear knocks at the door,
send faith to answer!*

———■———

Doubt has never changed anything.
Belief changes things.

———■———

Walk softly, speak tenderly,
and pray fervently.

———■———

Let your life story be for God's glory.

———■———

When you get to your wit's end,
you'll find God lives there.

———■———

When I have nothing left but God,
then I find that God is all I need.

———■———

We are never worthless, but unworthy.

———■———

*Faith produces a way of life
that pleases God.*

———■———

*If you want your life to be a
reflection of Christ, you need to
take time to reflect on Christ.*

———■———

*A faith worth having is
a faith worth sharing.*

———■———

*If you sense your faith is unraveling,
go back to where you dropped
the thread of obedience.*

———■———

*Faith is like an umbrella;
it protects us through the storms of life.*

———■———

45

*Faith gives us the courage to face
the present with confidence and
the future with expectancy.*

F-A-I-T-H: Forsaking all, I trust him.

---

*Be faithful
and leave the results to God.*

---

*If you are true to your faith,
there are things you give up
for your faith.*

---

*We should not put a question mark
where God puts a period.*

Wherever we go, God is there.
Whenever we call, God is listening.
Whatever we need, God is enough.

———■———

Every moment of worry weakens
the soul for its daily combat.

———■———

When you find time on your hands,
put them together in prayer.

———■———

Know the Bible in your head,
stow it in your heart, show it in
your life, sow it in the world.

———■———

Do not ask the Lord to guide your footsteps
if you are not willing to move your feet.

———■———

*The future is as bright as
the promises of God.*

———■———

*Every miracle Jesus does
starts with a problem.*

———■———

*Put everything in God's hand
and eventually you will see
God's hand in everything.*

———■———

Worry ends where faith begins.

———■———

*God meant for the Bible
to be bread for our daily use,
not just cake for special occasions.*

———■———

If God brings you to it,
he will bring you through it.

———■———

Prayers go up, blessings come down.

———■———

All our tomorrows must pass before God
before they ever reach us.

———■———

The closer you walk with God,
the less room for anything to come between.

———■———

Courage is faith singing in the rain.

———■———

Faith makes things possible, not easy.

———■———

*Faith is like stepping out at God's command
onto what appears to be a cloud
and finding it to be solid rock.*

---

*Love is the reason behind
everything God does.*

---

*Faith rests on God, receives from God,
responds to God, relies on God.*

---

*We wouldn't long for heaven
if earth had only joy.*

---

*If you don't want the fruits of sin,
stay out of the devil's orchard.*

---

*If God calls you to be a missionary,
don't stoop to be a king.*

———————■———————

*Though you may ask God to do
something **for** you, he generally
wants to do something **in** you.*

———————■———————

*Christians must keep the gospel,
but not to themselves.*

———————■———————

*For faith to prosper it must
experience impossible situations.*

Children & Family

———■———

*A child can read a parent's character
before he can read the alphabet.*

———■———

In the Old Order Amish district in Indiana where Joe Wittmer was raised, the birth of a baby was greeted with love, joy, and "sweet coffee."

"*Siess Kaffi*," says Dr. Wittmer, "is what neighbors do when a new baby arrives. The mom is given a week or so to rest, then folks start coming by with a meal and to see the new baby. They all have 'sugar in their coffee.'"

Some say there is no better babyhood than that enjoyed by an Amish baby. The Amish baby is an integral part of the family from the moment of birth. Even when asleep, the infant is often held in someone's arms. The Amish rarely, if ever, use babysitters. It's customary to take the baby with them wherever the parents go, even to long church services.

Dr. Wittmer says he's never known of a time when the birth of a child is an unwelcomed event. "A baby means another corn husker, another cow-milker, but most of all, another God-fearing Amishman. The birth is always seen as a blessing of the Lord."

Children are considered a gift from God, and family size attests to that: the average Amish family has seven children. Parents practice no birth control and pray for children. With such a high birthrate, the Amish have become the fastest growing population in the United States. As of 2009, the Young Center for Anabaptist and Pietist Studies at Elizabethtown College in Pennsylvania calculated there are over 233,000 Amish.[1] Over half the population is under eighteen years of age.

"Children are the poor man's wealth," says one proverb.

If faith is the cornerstone of Amish society, the home is the foundation. Marriage among the Amish is highly esteemed, and raising a family is like a professional career for adults. Divorce is virtually unheard of. One father wrote in *Family Life* magazine, "Children have only one childhood. We can fail in business and oftentimes start over and make good. But if we fail in the teaching and training of our children, we never get another chance."

Being family-centered is a long-held and deeply cherished Amish standard. "I can't put into words all that a home means to the Amish," says Dr. Wittmer. "It's almost something too deep for words. Family is number one." While in his *Rumspringa* (a term used for adolescence that is translated as "running around"), Joe Wittmer found the game of basketball. He went to high school, then to college. "I didn't go to get an education but to play basketball," he says. "I always had a plan to go back." But the path he started on led him to graduate school, where he eventually earned a doctorate in counseling psychology.

Does he regret leaving his heritage? "Would I trade? No. But I've always had that void."

Dr. Wittmer remains in close touch with his family. He was never baptized as a church member, thus he was not excommunicated. Today, he lives in Florida, but when he returns to Indiana, a large family reunion is held for him. "Over one hundred people," he says with a grin. "Everyone brings a dish. They all come."

Amish roots are strong, much more so than in contemporary American families. Many Amish live within several miles of their childhood homes. A typical Amish child may have two dozen aunts and uncles living in the area, plus dozens of cousins. Extended families are a blessing to each other and often live on the same piece of land.

"Youth likes to play, and old age to scold" sounds like something the middle-aged generation might mutter under their breath after a long day.

Sharing concern for a child's upbringing is a chief benefit of growing up in a thick network of extended family. "Parents and grandparents," says Laura Mast, an elderly Amish woman with fifty-two grandchildren and counting, "have the biggest job in the world. We have to teach the young to love the Lord." Properly raised children ensure a bright future for the Amish. These children will one day provide a home for their aging parents, as Laura's son and daughter-in-law are now doing for her.

What's Laura's best child-rearing advice? She answers with these proverbs: *"Children need models more than critics"* and *"Children live what they learn and learn what they live."* Another, she says, is *"Always treat children in the direction you wish them to grow, not as they now are."*

But even more important than providing an Amish-style social security, parents' greatest desire for their children is to share their hope for a heaven-bound future. One proverb that Erik Wesner, author of the popular blog *Amish America*, often hears is "Our children are the only treasures we can take to heaven."

A house is made of walls and beams;
a home is made of love and dreams.

A wife will make or break a household.

Summer is the season
when children slam the doors
they left open all winter.

Put the swing where the children want it.
The grass will grow back.

A father ought to help his son to form the habit of doing right on his own initiative rather than out of fear of serious consequences.

———■———

More is caught than taught.

———■———

Raising boys is as easy as digesting iron.

———■———

If you let your children have their own way, you must not complain if they give you trouble.

———■———

The most important things in your home are people.

———■———

*Tomorrow's world will be shaped by
what we teach our children today.*

———■———

Keep your feet under your own table.

———■———

*If parents don't train their children,
the children will train the parents.*

———■———

*There's a peg for every hole
and a lid for every pot.*

———■———

*A happy home is not merely having
a roof over your head but having
a foundation under your feet.*

———■———

Hands build houses, love builds homes.

———◼———

Children are natural imitators.
They act just like their parents in spite of
the effort to teach them good manners.

———◼———

A man needs a woman to take care
of him so she can make him strong
enough for her to lean on.

———◼———

Relationships are fragile,
handle with prayer.

———◼———

A child will not inherit his parents'
talents, but he will inherit their values.

———◼———

*Children's ears may be closed to advice,
but their eyes are open to examples.*

———————■———————

*A mother is a gardener of God tending
to the hearts of her children.*

———————■———————

*Your children are the heirs of your lifestyle,
your daily witness to your values.*

———————■———————

Bend the tree while it is a twig.

———————■———————

*The right temperature at home is
maintained by warm hearts, not hot heads.*

———————■———————

A mother's patience is like a tube of toothpaste. It's never quite gone.

———■———

Mothers write on the hearts of their children what the world's rough hand cannot erase.

———■———

To lead your children in the right way, you must go that way yourself.

———■———

Your companions are like buttons on an elevator: they will either take you up or down.

———■———

A grandmother is a little bit parent, a little bit teacher, and a little bit best friend.

———■———

The values we leave our children
are more important than the
valuables we leave them.

Mother makes dinner but
God makes the night.

Don't pour out the child with his bath.

When children are little
you have them in your lap;
when grown up,
on the heart.

Love a child, chastise him.

The burned child is afraid of fire.

———■———

A broken home is the world's greatest wreck.

———■———

*Every father should remember
that someday his sons
will follow his example
instead of his advice.*

———■———

*The family that works together,
eats together, and prays together,
stays together.*

———■———

*The best fathers not only give us life—
they teach us how to live.*

———■———

*A father's love is a feeling of security
in turbulent and busy times.*

*If we have perfect parents,
we would not have a need for God.*

*The apple will not roll far
away from its tree.*

There's a black sheep in every family.

Such a father, such a son.

*Before you question your husband's
judgment, consider who he married.*

In Word & Deed

---

*The person who thinks too little
usually talks too much.*

Edna is a soft-spoken, gracious woman in her nineties. Born and raised in Ohio, she was the eldest in a large Amish family. "I never heard my parents use the words 'I love you,'" she says. "But I knew they did. It just wasn't the Plain way. It wasn't until I married [a non-Amish man] that I started to use those words. It was difficult at first, even to tell my own children I loved them." She looks up. "But I think they knew that I did."

Her daughter, Judy, is by her side, bobbing her head in agreement. "We knew, Mom."

A theme in Amish life is to live by example, not by words. Expressions of sentiment are rare, not necessarily because the Amish don't have deep feelings, but because it seems worldly to air one's emotions. Words are not cheap to the Amish. *"Where water is deepest, it is stillest"* best sums it up.

Threaded throughout many Amish sayings is a great emphasis on filtering one's speech: *"You can't hang a man for his thoughts, but you mustn't think too loud."* Careless talk and gossip are frowned upon. *"Think ten times, talk once,"* or *"What one is ashamed to do one should be ashamed to say."* Or here's one that makes you wonder about who coined it and why: *"A woman's tongue is the last thing about her that dies."*

To the Amish, how a person acts says more about their faith than what they say they believe. The lack of emphasis Plain People place on evangelism is often misunderstood. Setting an example of a holy life, they feel, makes a better witness than mere talk. Rather than proselytize, the Amish provide practical help when natural disasters strike.

For example, busloads of young Amish men from the Lancaster area traveled to Pass Christian, Mississippi, to help rebuild homes after Hurricane Katrina. To their way of thinking, *"You can preach a better sermon with your life than with your lips."*

The messages behind "Actions speak louder than words" or "Kind actions begin with kind thoughts" seem so ordinary that we almost pass them by—but we shouldn't. Think of the impact of a good deed or a kind word. *"Good deeds have echoes."*

There's a biblical proverb behind this way of thinking: "Your own soul is nourished when you are kind; it is destroyed when you are cruel" (Prov. 11:17 LB). What is a nourished soul? It's one that feels inner joy and peace. Not smugness or pride or self-righteousness, but a deep-down awareness that you are doing the work of God.

The Amish believe that we are made in the image of a God who is by nature *good*. Doing good *is* God's work.

To quote an Amish scribe in *The Budget*, "*God doesn't ask us to be successful, only faithful.*"[1]

A fault mender is better than a fault finder.

An unkind remark is like a killing frost—no matter how much it warms up, the damage is already done.

Whoever talks about others will also talk of you.

He talks much when the day is long.

It's easy to talk if you're not in those shoes.

To belittle is to be little.

———■———

Talking won't fill the belly.

———■———

Some people are like buttons,
popping off at the wrong time.

———■———

A smile is a curve that can
straighten out a lot of things.

———■———

All that you do,
do with your might.
Things done by halves
are never done right.

———■———

*Swallowing words before you
say them is so much better than
having to eat them afterward.*

———■———

*When you speak, always remember
that God is one of your listeners.*

———■———

*To mistreat God's creation is
to offend the Creator.*

———■———

Repeating hearsay brings dismay.

———■———

*One way to save face is to keep
the lower half of it shut.*

———■———

*The best helping hand is the one
at the end of your arm.*

———■———

*Politeness is to do and say the
kindest thing in the kindest way.*

———■———

*It is easier to preach a sermon
than to live one.*

———■———

*Even though you can hide from
the earth, heaven sees you act.*

———■———

*Cut h off of "habit" and you will have "a bit"
left. Cut off a and you still have a "bit." Cut
off bit and you will have "it" conquered.*

———■———

Why is it so hard to say "I broke it"
and so easy to say "it broke"?

———————

Kind words and kind deeds keep
life's garden free of weeds.

———————

It takes 73 muscles to frown and
only 14 to smile. No wonder grouchy
people are always tired.

———————

To overcome sin, starve the old
nature and feed the new.

———————

A person who gets all wrapped up in
himself makes a mighty small package.

———————

71

He talked much but said little.

Three are too many to keep a secret.

---

*Open your ears to God before you
open your mouth to others.*

---

*A gossip can't be telling the truth all the
time—there isn't that much truth.*

---

*Great ideas don't seem to come
from swelled heads.*

Good intentions spoil if not used.

If you find it difficult to stand for
what's right, try kneeling first.

———■———

Think all you speak, but
speak not all you think.

———■———

When we give others a piece of our mind,
we have no peace left.

———■———

Beware of your thoughts; they may
become words any minute.

———■———

Advice is like cooking.
You should try it
before you feed it to others.

———■———

*Deal with the faults of others
as gently as your own.*

———■———

*Be slow to anger and quick to forgive, and
you will have friends for as long as you live.*

———■———

*It takes some folks a long time to tell
you they have nothing to say.*

———■———

*A negative attitude is like a flat tire.
You won't get very far without changing it.*

———■———

*If you cannot be thankful for what
you have received, be thankful
for what you have escaped.*

———■———

*The best way to have the last
word is to apologize.*

———■———

*Four things never return: the spoken
word, the sped arrow, past life,
and neglected opportunity.*

———■———

*The easiest way to make a mountain
out of a molehill is to add a little dirt.*

———■———

*Words break no bones,
but they can break hearts.*

———■———

*What other people think of you
is none of your business.*

Work Ethic

A good name, like good will, is earned
by many actions and lost by one.

The *Washington Post* ran a story about a woman in southern Maryland who wanted to have a modular house built.[1] She asked friends and relatives for a recommendation for a good contractor. She finally settled on one: an Amish builder with an excellent reputation. She drove out to the builder's farm (since he was Amish, he had no phone) and described to him the kind of house she wanted. Happily, she agreed to the price tag he gave her, far lower than she had expected. In fact, commercial builders had quoted two to three times the price of the Amish builder.

But there were two parts of the arrangement that shocked her. One was the builder's waiting list: two years. The other was that there was no contract, no deposit required. Only a handshake to seal the deal. The transaction was based on trust.

If there is one characteristic the Amish are admired for, it is their strong work ethic. The Amish brand sells. It's even become a source of controversy as non-Amish businesses try to capitalize on the brand by labeling their products as Amish ones. "A general rule of thumb," says Erik Wesner, a scholar who studies the Amish and runs the *Amish America* blog, "is that if it *says* Amish, then it ain't."

Instilling a work ethic starts at a young age. Teaching a child to work and accept responsibility is one of the most important traits Amish parents hope to instill in their children. Traditional sayings strongly emphasize the renowned Amish work ethic:

He that cometh first to the
mill, grindeth first.

———■———

The morning hour has gold in hand,
woe to those who heed it not.

Perseverance is encouraged: *"If you don't give up, you haven't lost."*

An Amish child begins "choring" at the age of four or five, and the care of farm animals plays a big role in teaching daily responsibility. Boys and girls learn to feed chickens, gather eggs, and bottle nurse the calf. At a later age, most children are given charge of an animal—usually a calf or heifer—that will become exclusively theirs. The fate of the animal is linked to the care and attention it is given. The child learns the direct consequences of feeding, growth, birth, breeding . . . or neglect and disease. And in the natural course of events, they learn about death too. "He cares more about the wool than he does about the sheep" is an insult. It says that how an individual treats animals can unmask the truth about his character to others.

After Amish teenagers leave school at eighth grade and begin working, they customarily give their paychecks to their parents until they marry or turn 21. Parents provide a small allowance and bank the remainder. When a child marries, most parents will then help with the purchase of a farm or the start-up of a business. Amish parents believe that too much money at too young an age only leads to temptations. *"Give the child a finger and he will want the whole hand"* is an old-fashioned way of saying that providing too much can de-motivate a child. Here's another one: *"Give a child his will, and a whelp his fill, and neither will thrive."*

Laziness ranks as a cardinal sin. *"Yes, tomorrow and not today, is what all lazy people say."* *"A lazy donkey will work itself to death sooner than a busy one"* is another way of saying that laziness kills quicker than activity. *"A lazy sheep thinks its wool heavy"* describes a person who can't take care of their own obligations.

Let's turn this around. While laziness is a disgrace, working hard—with integrity and honesty—is a cherished characteristic, even if these qualities cause a person to be taken advantage of by others. The Amish live by the proverbs *"It is better to suffer wrong than to commit wrong"* and *"A man is happier to be sometimes cheated than to never trust."* If they are wronged, so be it. They will not fight in wars. They will not sue anyone in a court of law. To the Amish way of thinking, vengeance belongs to God. They conduct modern business the old-fashioned way—with a hand-shake, a word of honor, and trust.

One stroke fells not an oak.

———■———

*A truly happy person is one who can
enjoy the scenery of a detour.*

———■———

*Advice when most needed
is least heeded.*

———■———

*Those who can't forget are worse
than those who can't remember.*

———■———

A heart at peace gives life to the body.

———■———

*Those who fear the future are
likely to fumble the present.*

———■———

A bird is known by its feathers.

———■———

*The soundness of your ideas is more
important than the sound of your words.*

———■———

Don't believe everything you think!

———■———

*It is better to give others a piece of your
heart than a piece of your mind.*

———■———

*The key to contentment is to realize
life is a gift—not a right.*

———■———

81

A man should not grieve overmuch,
for that is a complaint against God.

———■———

No mill, no meat.

———■———

No pains, no gains.

———■———

They must hunger in frost that
will not work in heat.

———■———

Harvest comes not every day.

———■———

Don't spend a dollar to save a penny.

———■———

*Contentment is not getting what we want
but being satisfied with what we have.*

————■————

*People who reject law and order
change their minds when they can lay
down the laws and give the orders.*

————■————

*If you put your finger to the fire,
it will get burned.*

————■————

You don't need to get sick to get better.

————■————

*God's best is known by
surrender—not struggle.*

————■————

*Contentment and trust are
characteristics of a sanctified life.*

———■———

*If we don't stand for something,
we will fall for anything.*

———■———

Half done is far from done.

———■———

Everything begun but nothing done.

———■———

*Every bird pipes according
to the shape of its bill.*

———■———

*If you can't see the bright side,
polish the dull.*

———■———

God has work for all his children,
regardless of age or ability.

———■———

You cannot be truly a son of God
without resembling the Father.

———■———

The trouble with doing nothing is it's
too hard to tell when you're finished.

———■———

Pride in your work puts joy in your day.

———■———

The laborer is worthy of his hire.

———■———

The one thing that is worse than a quitter
is the man who is afraid to begin.

———■———

85

*If you want life's best, see to it
that life gets your best.*

———■———

The laborer's fare always tastes sweetest.

———■———

Oiled machinery runs smooth.

———■———

The last cow closes the door.

———■———

*No man can do nothing and no
man can do everything.*

———■———

*The lazier a man is, the more
he's going to do tomorrow.*

———■———

*Common sense is often wisdom
clothed in work clothes.*

———■———

Burying your talents is a grave mistake.

———■———

*The person who says it can't be done
should not interrupt the person doing it.*

———■———

A man must walk before he can run.

———■———

Fortune favors the bold.

———■———

As the work, so the pay.

———■———

*Everyone must carry his own
hide to the tanner.*

———————————————

What costs little is little esteemed.

———————————————

*If everyone sweeps before his own door,
the whole street would be clean.*

———————————————

Don't hitch the cart before the horse.

———————————————

A thin meadow is soon mowed.

———————————————

*Many people fail to recognize opportunity
because it comes disguised as work.*

———————————————

Excuses are the nails that hold
together the house of failure.

———■———

The right train of thought can take
you to a better station in life.

———■———

If you don't have time to do a
job right, you're going to have
to make time to do it over.

———■———

Pray for a good harvest but continue to hoe.

———■———

Rust ruins more tools than overuse does.

———■———

Even a woodpecker has found
the way to progress is to use your head.

Handling Adversity

The higher the mountain,
the deeper the valley.

In late November 2008, Daniel Troyer was told by his doctors that he needed surgery to repair a valve in his heart. The surgery took place a few weeks later. The very next morning, an icy and cold December day, Daniel's eight-year-old grandson was hit by a car as he walked to school. He was killed instantly.

Later that week, still recovering, Daniel was able to attend his grandson's funeral. The Old Order Amish bishop concluded the service by saying not once, not twice, but three times, "God always has a plan."

The Amish believe that God is sovereign over this world—everyone and everything in it. "Adversity is just part of life, and you cope with adversity by accepting it," says Dr. Joe Wittmer, author of *The Gentle People: An Inside View of Amish Life*. Such yielding to God's will is a distinctive Amish trait.

Non-Amish Christians typically (maybe not accurately, but typically) believe that their faith will deliver them *from* adversity. The Amish believe they will be delivered *in* adversity. When bad things happen, they don't question if God exists or why he would allow such a thing. "That does not mean that they do not grieve a death, for example, but their grief always seems lighter to me," says Dr. Wittmer. "Maybe because it is shared by the entire community. An individual really has no control over adversity or much of anything else, for that matter."

A traditional saying that means no one can tell what a day may bring forth is *"Hale at morn and dead by night."*

Rather than question God's ways—which the Amish would perceive as prideful—they strengthen their faith by dwelling on God's character and the hope for eternity. Notice in these sayings how the focus is on God's provision to endure a difficult circumstance:

God is there to give us strength for
every hill we have to climb.

Never doubt in the dark what God
has shown you in the light.

Trusting God turns problems into opportunities.

The Amish are no strangers to adversity. They are descendants of European Anabaptists, who in the late sixteenth century were the radicals of the day, persecuted and martyred for their beliefs. A secret police force of "Anabaptist hunters" was organized to spy on, locate, and arrest Anabaptists for their nonconformist beliefs. The Amish found refuge in remote parts of France, Switzerland, and Germany, and farmed land that no one else wanted. Even today, at every church service, they sing centuries-old hymns that recall those days of persecution.

With such a background of hardships, self-sufficiency became a core value for the Amish. Today they don't purchase insurance policies, they don't accept any government subsidies or pensions (though they do pay taxes), they don't send their children to public school.

"It's your own fault if you leave the table hungry" or *"When the cover is short, you must pull up your legs"* reflect the attitude that the Amish don't expect this world to cater to them. In a matter-of-fact way, they expect the rain to fall on the just and the unjust: *"This is the way of the world—one has the stockings, the other the shoes."*

But the Amish do take care of their own. Mutual aid is provided to help in times of medical or financial difficulties. The barn raising might be the best metaphor to illustrate how the Amish handle adversity. When a barn burns down, they don't dwell on why it burned, they gather together to rebuild. And then they praise God: for the lumber, the nails, the caring community that skillfully puts it together, the animals that will inhabit it, and for a chance to start again.

*God won't lead you where his
grace can't keep you.*

———■———

*Lightning doesn't strike every
time it thunders.*

———■———

*Hope for the best, prepare for the worst,
and take what comes with a smile.*

———■———

*Nothing is all wrong: even a clock that
has stopped running is right twice a day.*

———■———

*Someday the scales of justice
will be perfectly balanced.*

———■———

There are lots of ways to cut a cake.

Learn from your failures,
or you will fail to learn.

The best way to escape evil
is to pursue good.

Just when the caterpillar thought the
world was over, it became a butterfly.

We value the light more fully after
we've come through the darkness.

95

*You can never tell which way the
train went by looking at the tracks.*

———————■———————

*God could save us from trauma, but
instead he sends us a Comforter.*

———————■———————

*Instead of complaining that the
rosebush is full of thorns, be glad
that the thornbush has roses.*

———————■———————

*Life can be compared to rowing across a
swift stream. We must continue our efforts
of paddling against the current, or we
shall drift downstream to the rocks and
rapids and not reach the other shore.*

———————■———————

*All the water in the world cannot sink
our boat as long as it's on the outside.*

———————■———————

Be like the teakettle; when it's up to
its neck in hot water, it sings.

———■———

You can tell when you're on the
right track. It's usually uphill.

———■———

Defeat isn't bitter if you don't swallow it.

———■———

Forgiveness withheld is like drinking poison
and waiting for the offender to die.

———■———

God wants to use you stumbling and
all, but he can't if you refuse to get up.

———■———

The anvil outlasts the hammer.

———■———

97

*No clouds are so dark that God
cannot see through them.*

———■———

*When once a dog has killed a sheep, it will
be blamed for the death of every sheep.*

———■———

Even a clever hen will lay outside the nest.

———■———

*Gray hairs do not weigh any
heavier than the rest.*

———■———

*Some may see a hopeless end, but as
believers we rejoice in an endless hope.*

———■———

*Greatness lies not in trying to be somebody
but in trying to help somebody.*

---

*In order to mold his people, God
often has to melt them.*

---

*If you removed the rocks, the
brook would lose its song.*

---

*Heaven's delights will far
outweigh earth's difficulties.*

---

*Adversity reveals character;
prosperity hides it.*

No house without a mouse, no barn
without corn, no rose without a thorn.

———■———

No burden so great as that
which is self-made.

———■———

A long life hath long miseries.

———■———

You can never tell where the trouble lies.

———■———

Life is not a problem to be solved
but a gift to be enjoyed.

———■———

If you aren't happy today, what
day are you waiting for?

———■———

*A hen does not quit scratching just because
the worms are scarce. She scratches
that much more to make her living.*

---

*Those who bless God in their trials will
be blessed by God through their trials.*

---

*Patience is accepting a difficult situation,
without giving God a deadline to remove it.*

God orders our stops as well as our steps.

Poor or rich, death levels all.

Education

No man is his craft's master the first day.

Naomi Weaver grew up in Holmes County, Ohio, in a large Amish family. In September of 1962, as the new school year started up, Naomi's father decided she had enough public schooling and kept her home. Her birthday was in the fall, anyway. So what's a month or two?

The truant officer held a different point of view. He paid a visit to Naomi's home with a police officer and had her father arrested. Naomi's father spent a day in the county jail.

"After that," Naomi said, "I went to school every day! Until I turned sixteen. Then, happily, I quit." Naomi laughed at the memory but admitted it wasn't so funny when her dad was taken away in a police car.

Although the Amish are peaceable people, they can be surprisingly stubborn. There are some areas that they will not budge on. Take, for example, higher education. *"Rub up against a black kettle and you will become black"* summarizes the Amish view of public education.

For the first half of the twentieth century, Amish children attended public schools. For most of rural America, that consisted of one-room schoolhouses. Under local control, these schools posed little threat to Amish values. But the massive consolidation of public schools after World War II sparked clashes between the Amish and state officials—such as the one Naomi's dad faced. After legal skirmishes in several states, the United States Supreme Court gave the green light to the eighth-grade Amish school system in 1972, permitting Amish youth to complete formal schooling at the age of fourteen.

Small, parochial schools are critically important to the Amish; they help preserve the culture by reinforcing values and insulating "scholars" from contaminating worldly ideas. These one-room schools prepare children for meaningful lives in Amish society by teaching cooperation, responsibility, hard work, and basic skills for living. Their goal is to support Amish ways.

"If education is to be judged by its achievements, the Amish may have one of the most effective instructional systems in the world today," writes Dr. Joe Wittmer.[1]

Though the classroom work ends at the eighth grade, an Amish education carries on at home. Children continue to learn trades and homemaking skills, all steeped in the same ethics of working hard and responsibly. In fact, much of the Amish educational process takes place at home. Amish parents believe it is their obligation—not the state's—to educate their children. School and church are an extension of home; however, the chief models of the Amish culture are Mom and Dad.

The Amish have a suspicion about higher education. *"He knoweth much who knows that he knows nothing"* or *"He who knows least hast most to say"* or *"Those who hold their heads too high haven't much in 'em"* reflect a disdain for the pridefulness that the Amish believe often accompanies higher education.

Don't misunderstand. The Amish highly regard learning—but not for its own sake. Education is purposeful, and experience makes for the best teacher. *"Experience keeps a dear school, but fools learn in no other,"* one proverb explains. The Amish value learning by doing and are remarkably adept at finding specific information to learn a new skill. Because they have no exposure to other media, the Amish spend much more time reading than most Americans. Illiteracy is virtually nonexistent.

"Being lifelong learners is very important to them," says Dr. Wittmer. "They have to learn new skills all the time. They've learned how to work hard since they were young children. They've gotten up in the cold with a lantern to milk the cows at 4 a.m. That's the way they've done it, they still work hard. They apply that same work ethic to learning new skills."

Walnut Creek, Ohio, is home to Carlisle Press, a small Amish-run printing company. The owner adds this message to the back of each book: "Marvin Wengerd is a member of the Amish and he represents one of the many young Amish entrepreneurs who are developing new businesses apart from farming while at the same time remaining faithful to their Amish traditions. He and the employees of his company are dedicated to producing a quality product for their customers. They are mostly self-taught in the printing business and continue to expand their knowledge about printing."

Learning, for the Amish, is not attached to a report card or SATs or getting into the right college. Learning is attached to life.

Knowledge is the power of the mind.
Wisdom is the power of the soul.

———

Young folks should use their
ears and not their mouths.

———

Learning is far more valuable
than education.

———

Some read just enough to keep
themselves misinformed.

———

Experience keeps a dear school,
but fools learn in no other.

———■———

Experience costs gold.

———■———

Remember, when you talk, you only
repeat what you already know; if you
listen, you might learn something.

———■———

One can learn something new every day.

———■———

Knowledge is power, but like power, it
must be hitched to something effective.

———■———

Take a fancy to a thing or you can't learn it.

———■———

You're never too old to learn.

You can't get no learnin' in an armchair.

A man cannot be robbed of his learning.

*Whoever acquires knowledge but
does not practice it is like one who
plows a field but does not sow it.*

*Instruction may end in the classroom,
but education ends only with life.*

*Strange how much we've got to know
before we know how little we know.*

Experience is a hard teacher. She gives the test first, then the lesson afterward.

A good teacher works to capture a student's attention so he can direct it toward God.

Today—read a sound book, think a good thought, live a blessed life.

That person is truly wise who gains his wisdom from the experience of others, thereby saving himself from learning by experience.

Children's ears may be closed to advice, but their eyes are open to examples.

It is easy to learn what you like.

———■———

Easy to learn, soon forgotten.

———■———

The first step to wisdom: Silence.
The second step: Listen.

Community

*The only time to look down on
your neighbor is when you're
bending over to help.*

When Judy, a sixty-something woman with salt-and-pepper hair, was diagnosed with breast cancer, she faced a rigorous schedule of surgery and radiation. Her husband, friends, and neighbors were with her each step of the way. Her husband attended every doctor's appointment and kept a notebook filled with detailed notes of what the doctor said, so they could refer back to it at home. Her friends brought meals after the surgery and on radiation days and prayed daily for her recovery.

"Having everyone's support and practical help felt like the warm blanket you get wrapped up with after surgery," says Judy. "The circumstances of having cancer hadn't changed, but the love and care of others helped me get through it."

People need people. Everyone needs a community. Isn't that what is behind the exploding success of social networks such as Facebook and Twitter? People seeking people. We have a longing to be needed and to belong to something bigger than ourselves. It's just the way God wired us. The sayings *"No one is strong enough to bear his burdens alone"* and *"Compassion puts love into action"* reflect Judy's experience.

Most people think of community as a place, a geographical location. In reality—for Amish or non-Amish—communities are much more than a physical place. They are the world where people live, work, raise their children, and go to church.

Community is an extremely important aspect of Amish life because the Amish's religious values emphasize the importance of living together as a body of believers. It's one of the reasons the Amish remain tied to the horse and buggy—it creates an invisible boundary. They need to live in close proximity to each other to maintain face-to-face contact with family, friends, and neighbors. Even the size of the church district is kept intentionally small so that all members are within one hour's ride of each other. When a church district gets too large to accommodate members in a home (the Amish worship in homes), it will divide into two.

The Amish world revolves around a local turf. The same people frequently work, play, and worship together. They join together to help raise a barn, to sew a quilt, to build a new schoolhouse, and then to maintain it.

"After a threshing frolic [a work party to help a farmer thresh his crop]," says Dr. Joe Wittmer, who was raised in an Old Order Amish home, "we'd have a thresher meeting to settle up. If one farmer had help for three days and another for four, he'd pay up for that extra person. It was a time of celebration, that the crops were in. And we'd always have homemade ice cream."

With each event, Amish people attach more deeply as a community, belonging in a way beyond measure. Such is the saying *"People with a heart for God have a heart for people."*

The Amish live together, worship together, socialize together. They help each other—as friends, neighbors, relatives, all members of a church district. Community, for the Amish, is not made from a place. Community is made up of familiar faces and helping hands.

Love enables us to walk fearlessly,
to run confidently,
and to live victoriously.

———■———

Community is like an old coat—
you aren't aware of it until it is taken away.

———■———

The best vitamin for making friends is B$_1$.

———■———

113

*It is better to hold out a helping
hand than to point a finger.*

———■———

We cannot catch our neighbor's foxes.

———■———

Two cannot quarrel when one will not.

———■———

Tackle the problem, not the person.

———■———

Cheerfulness greases the axles of the world.

———■———

A small leak will sink a large ship.

———■———

*Too many people limit their exercise to
jumping to conclusions, running up bills,
stretching the truth, bending over backward,
lying down on the job, sidestepping
responsibility, and pushing their luck.*

---

*A friend is never known till
a man has a need.*

Develop a forgiving attitude.

---

*We can stop forgiving others when
Christ stops forgiving us.*

---

*Our duty is not to see through one another,
but to see one another through.*

If you listen through the wall,
you'll hear others reciting your faults.

———■———

Details beget more details.

———■———

Love always finds a home in
the heart of a friend.

———■———

The waves of hatred beat in vain
against the rock of love.

———■———

Prosper and you'll have lots of friends.

———■———

Those who are to get together
will get together.

———■———

Love will find a way.

———■———

Two heads are better than one.

———■———

Let every man alone
and you'll be let alone.

———■———

Watch a person as a cat does a mouse.

———■———

Howl with the wolves or they
will tear you to pieces.

———■———

Go far from home and you will
have a long way back.

———■———

When it comes to doing things for others,
some people stop at nothing.

———■———

Mentioning the faults of others
does not rid us of our own.

———■———

There is no greater love than the
love that holds on where there
seems nothing left to hold on to.

———■———

Before you flare up at anyone's faults,
take time to count to ten—
ten of your own.

———■———

The person who sows seeds of kindness
will have a perpetual harvest.

———■———

Don't let anger fester for too long.
Make the first move toward reconciliation.

He who talks to you about others
will talk to others about you.

Swallowing pride rarely
gives you indigestion.

Many things have been opened by mistake,
but none so frequently as the mouth.

Friendship is a plant which
must often be watered.

119

*Love's power to forgive is stronger
than hate's power to get even.*

———■———

*Love God completely, love others
compassionately, love yourself correctly.*

———■———

*People who care about each other
take care of one another.
It's not a duty, it's a pleasure.*

———■———

*Freedom is not the right to do as you
please but the liberty to do as you ought.*

———■———

*Tiny snowflakes sticking together
can accomplish great things.*

———■———

*A Christian without a church is
like a bee without a hive.*

―――――――― ▪ ――――――――

*A song coupled with service
makes a beautiful sermon.*

―――――――― ▪ ――――――――

*If you won't admit you've been wrong,
you love yourself more than truth.*

―――――――― ▪ ――――――――

*Indignation is the poison we
drink to kill our friends.*

―――――――― ▪ ――――――――

*May our lives be like arithmetic:
friends added, enemies subtracted,
sorrows divided, joys multiplied.*

―――――――― ▪ ――――――――

121

*The only people with whom you
should try to get even are those
who have been kind to you.*

———————■———————

*Apple butter, just like relationships,
takes time to boil, time to cool, and
time to turn out wonderfully.*

———————■———————

*There is a vast difference between
putting your nose in other people's
business and putting your heart
in other people's problems.*

———————■———————

*When you dig another out of their troubles,
you find a place to bury your own.*

———————■———————

*The real secret of happiness is not what you
give or what you receive, it's what you share.*

Character

Friendships cemented together with sin do not hold.

There's a beautiful body of water in England called Mill Pond, where swans frequently make a stop on their annual migration. Stretched across one corner of the pond are overhead power lines. A number of swans have been killed because they didn't see the power lines as they approached the pond to make a landing. After neighbors complained, the power company installed red flags on the lines. The swans, now alerted to the danger, avoid the lines. Since the red flags were installed, not a single swan has died.

Proverbs are meant to act like those red flags that were provided for the swans' protection. With enough repetition, the Amish principles of simple living should pop into a person's mind when he sees danger ahead. The Amish understand a biblical truth: paths that lead to sin—like those power lines—can be nearly invisible, yet have devastating consequences to one's character.

Maintaining a person's character begins—and continues—with a decision, so these red flags create "advanced decision making." Under pressure, a well-developed character can stand firm and respond by knowing God's way. The best way. Tempted to lie to get out of a tight spot? Up pops the red flag: "The LORD detests lying lips" (Prov. 12:22). Decision made! Such principles of wisdom have been so engrained through repetitive use of proverbs and sayings that, when one is faced with a critical crossroad in daily life, vital messages trumpet out good judgment.

Easy to remember, proverbs can clarify the difference between right and wrong, good and evil; they help an individual avoid moral mud puddles. With rich and colorful language, these sayings evoke vivid word pictures:

"You can smell scorched soup from afar" is a reminder that gossip spreads like wildfire.

"Much straw but little grain" is a person who is all talk but no substance.

This one needs no explanation: *"They who trim themselves to suit others will soon whittle themselves away."*

The Amish believe that no one is born with an innately good character . . . and pride is every human being's "default button." It's where our natures tend to slip. Curiously, many common sayings have to do with a mule facing the consequences . . . of being mulish: *"Wherever an ass falleth, there will he never fall again"* means you can put a mule in a dilemma only once. Can't you just picture a father trying to teach his son to learn from a mistake and not repeat it?

Here's a favorite: *"'One must remember where it comes from,' said the farmer when the mule kicked him."* Wouldn't you love to know the story behind that one?

One of the main tasks of the Christian life is to grow out of folly and into wisdom. Wisdom flows from good character. But part of the process of developing a good character involves making mistakes. Many bromides take a tongue-in-cheek approach to life's mishaps.

"Every hen will lay an imperfect egg now and then" implies that accidents happen in the best of families. *"Even a clever hen will lay outside the nest"* means that everyone makes mistakes.

But a man who doesn't learn from his mistakes?

Well, as the saying goes, "He went through school like the mule through the mill; in at one end and out at the other."

Now *that* is cause for concern.

Good character like good soup
is usually homemade.

Remember that wherever
you go, there you are.

---

*Enthusiasm is contagious
and so is the lack of it.*

———■———

*A truly humble person
is not easily offended.*

———■———

*You can tell a man's character
by what he turns up when offered a job—
his nose or his sleeves.*

———■———

Don't crow too soon.

———■———

*You can look a man into the face
but not into the heart.*

———■———

Fat hens lay few eggs.

———◼———

*He who has never done anything wrong
has never done anything right.*

———◼———

Better to die honest than to live in disgrace.

———◼———

*Before asking for another talent,
be sure you make use of what you have.*

———◼———

*No one raises his own reputation
by lowering others.'*

———◼———

*Doing what's right today means
no regrets tomorrow.*

———◼———

*Contentment is discovering the value of
what God has already given to me.*

———■———

*Carry God's Word when you are young
and it will carry you when you are old.*

———■———

*Truth can be trampled to the ground,
but it will always stand back up.*

———■———

*Either the world is changing us
or we're changing the world.*

———■———

*To lead your children in the right way,
you must go that way yourself.*

———■———

Intelligence is like a river—
the deeper it is,
the less noise it makes.

———■———

The best way to succeed in life is to
act on the advice we give to others.

———■———

A good tree will not bear strange fruit.

———■———

We may face situations beyond our reserves
but never beyond God's resources.

———■———

An old sore is hard to heal.

———■———

*Courage is something you can never
lose, because courage is something
you can always choose.*

———————■———————

*You are richer today if you have
laughed, given, or forgiven.*

———————■———————

*The key ingredient to a great
loaf of bread is patience.*

———————■———————

A clear conscience is a soft pillow.

———————■———————

Straight ahead is shorter than round about.

———————■———————

Not all is gold that shines.

Just for Fun

If you are under the impression that the Amish don't have a sense of humor, well, "have another think" . . .

Every family tree has a little sap.

"Don't get caught" is the eleventh commandment.

If you get to be as old as a cow, you'll learn s'more anyhow.

The poor man sleeps soundly;
he need have no fear of thieves.

Better to break an arm than a neck.

Whoever is afraid of doing too much
always does least.

Those who have no children know
best how to raise them.

If the grass looks greener on
the other side, fertilize.

Short hair is quickly brushed.

---

*If you can swallow a pill while
drinking from a water fountain,
you deserve to get well.*

———————■———————

Kissing wears out, cooking don't.

———————■———————

*A woman's work is not seen
unless it's not done.*

———————■———————

*Nothing is quite so annoying
as to have someone go right on talking
when you are interrupting.*

———————■———————

*In the kingdom of the blind,
one-eyed men are kings.*

———————■———————

Don't sell a poor horse near home.

---

*The world has too many cranks
and not enough self-starters.*

---

*Sometimes elbow grease is the most
valuable tool in the kitchen.*

---

*Burn the candle by day and you'll
have to sit in the dark at night.*

---

*Doing nothing is the most tiresome
job in the world because it's
impossible to quit to take a rest.*

Even the devil does not know it all.

———◼———

Confidence is the feeling you have before
you fully understand the situation.

———◼———

If everything is coming your direction,
you are in the wrong lane.

———◼———

A wooden spoon compels even the strangest
of ingredients to get their acts together.

———◼———

An honest cook serves her food
with the burnt side up.

———◼———

Daylight saving time is based on the ancient idea of lengthening a blanket by cutting off one end and sewing it on the other end.

One of the best things to have up your sleeve is your funny bone.

Firewood heats you twice—once when you cut it and again when you burn it.

A perfectionist is someone who takes great pains and gives them to others.

Memory is that thing which reminds us we have forgotten something that we cannot remember.

Winter is the season where we keep the house as hot as it was last summer when we complained about it being too hot.

———————■———————

Marriages are made in heaven—but then so are thunder and lightning.

———————■———————

Few things have a shorter life span than a clean garage.

———————■———————

Middle age starts on the day you become more concerned with how far a horse will go rather than how fast.

———————■———————

By the time most folks get to greener pastures, they can't climb the fence.

———————■———————

There are three kinds of ignorant people—
ignorant, very ignorant, and
hopelessly ignorant.

Other people's food always taste best.

A stink is still worse for the stirring.

If you could know everything in advance,
you would soon be rich or crazy.

An old woman's dancing doesn't last long.

Even a cat may look upon a king.

Mice with the shortest tails
are soonest hidden.

———■———

A miss is as good as a mile.

———■———

Bacon and rind are of a one kind.

———■———

Moths always destroy the best.

———■———

A fox may grow gray but never good.

———■———

You can't hatch chickens from fried eggs.

Notes

Introduction: The Amish in Their Own Words

1. J. Vernon McGee, *Thru the Bible with J. Vernon McGee*, Volume III, Proverbs–Malachi (Nashville: Thomas Nelson, 1982), 1.

2. Edwin Miller Fogel, *Proverbs of the Pennsylvania Germans* (Millersville, PA: Center for Pennsylvania German Studies, 1995), v.

3. Email conversation with Dr. Kraybill, Summer 2009.

Time

1. Joe Wittmer, PhD, correspondence with author, Summer 2009.

Money

1. Annenberg Center for the Digital Future at University of Southern California (June 16, 2009), www.digitalcenter.org/pdf/cdf_family_time.pdf.

Children & Family

1. Young Center for Anabaptist and Pietist Studies at Elizabethtown College in Pennsylvania, http://www2.etown.edu/Population_Trends_2007-2008.asp.

In Word & Deed

1. *The Budget* (Sugarcreek, OH). Quote reprinted with permission from editor Fannie Erb-Miller.

Work Ethic

1. Philip Rucker, "Bullish on Amish-Built," *Washington Post*, February 1, 2007, www.washingtonpost.com/wp-dyn/content/article/2007/01/03/AR2007013101894.

Education

1. Joe Wittmer, PhD, *The Gentle People: An Inside View of Amish Life* (Washington, IN: Black Buggy, 2007), 149.

Suzanne Woods Fisher first became interested in the culture of the Plain People through her grandfather, W. D. Benedict, who was raised in the Old Order German Baptist Brethren Church (also known as Dunkards) in Franklin County, Pennsylvania. She has a warm relationship with her Dunkard cousins and asks them many, many questions, which they patiently answer. She is the bestselling author of *The Choice*, *The Waiting*, *The Search*, *The Keeper*, and *The Haven*, as well as nonfiction books about the Amish, including *Amish Peace*. She is also the coauthor of a new Amish children's series, The Adventures of Lily Lapp. Suzanne is the host of the internet radio show *Amish Wisdom* and a columnist for *Christian Post* and *Cooking & Such* magazines. She lives in California and loves to hear from her readers. Find her online at www.suzannewoodsfisher.com.